THE HISTORY OF THE INDIANAPOLIS COLTS

THE HISTORY OF THE
INDIANAPOLIS

Published by Creative Education
123 South Broad Street
Mankato, Minnesota 56001
Creative Education is an imprint of The Creative Company.

DESIGN AND PRODUCTION BY **EVANSDAY DESIGN**

LIBRARY OF CONGRESS CATALOGING-IN-PUBLICATION DATA

Hawkes, Brian (Brian F.)
The history of the Indianapolis Colts / by Brian Hawkes.
p. cm. — (NFL today)
Summary: An overview of the history of the professional football team,
the Indianapolis Colts.
ISBN 1-58341-299-9
1. Indianapolis Colts (Football team)—History—Juvenile literature. 2. Baltimore
Colts (Football team)—History—Juvenile literature.
[1. Indianapolis Colts (Football team)—History.
2. Baltimore Colts (Football team)—History. 3. Football—History.]
I. Title. II. Series.

GV956.I53H39 2004
796.332'64'0977252—dc22   2003062581

First edition

9 8 7 6 5 4 3 2 1

COVER PHOTO: running back Edgerrin James

WHEN THE CITY OF INDIANAPOLIS, INDIANA, WAS FOUNDED IN 1850, IT WAS HOME TO ABOUT 8,000 PEOPLE. SINCE THAT TIME, IT HAS GROWN INTO A CITY OF MORE THAN 700,000 PEOPLE. THE PEOPLE OF INDIANAPOLIS AND ALL OF INDIANA HAVE LONG LOVED SPORTS. THE UNIVERSITY OF INDIANA HOOSIERS ARE A COLLEGE BASKETBALL POWERHOUSE, AND PROFESSIONAL BASKETBALL'S INDIANA PACERS HAVE A PASSIONATE FOLLOWING. EVERY YEAR, THE CITY HOSTS THE INDIANAPOLIS 500, THE MOST FAMOUS AUTO RACE IN THE WORLD. SINCE 1984, INDIANAPOLIS HAS ALSO BEEN HOME TO A NATIONAL FOOTBALL LEAGUE (NFL) FRANCHISE CALLED THE COLTS. THE TEAM WAS ACTUALLY BORN IN BALTIMORE, MARYLAND, IN 1953 AND DREW ITS NAME FROM BALTIMORE'S GREAT HORSE RACING TRADITION. AFTER MOVING FROM THE EAST COAST TO AMERICA'S HEARTLAND, THE TEAM WITH THE HORSESHOE ON ITS HELMET QUICKLY EARNED A PLACE IN THE HEARTS OF INDIANA SPORTS FANS.

THE BALTIMORE COLTS played their first season in Baltimore in 1953 and were led early on by veteran NFL coach Weeb Ewbank. From 1953 to 1955, the Colts went a combined 11–24–1. Then, before the 1956 season, an un-known quarterback named Johnny Unitas was brought in for a tryout. The coaches were impressed enough with the tough young passer to add him to the team. Early in the 1956 season, Baltimore's starting quarterback broke his leg. Unitas stepped in and quickly established himself as a star with a knack for producing amazing comeback victories.

Unitas led the Colts to a 7–5 record in 1957. In 1958, Baltimore jumped to 9–3. By then the team had a high-powered offense that featured Unitas, bruising fullback Alan Ameche, and sure-handed receivers Lenny Moore and Raymond Berry. These players led the way as the young Colts charged all the way to the 1958 NFL championship game, where they faced the New York Giants.

With under two minutes left in that game, the Colts had the ball on their own 14-yard line trailing the Giants 17–14. Unitas guided the Colts into field goal range, and kicker Steve Myrha tied the game with just seconds remaining. For the first time in NFL history, the championship game went into sudden-death overtime. In overtime, Unitas worked his magic again. After the star quarterback moved the Colts to New York's two-yard line, Ameche plunged into the end zone to give the Colts a 23–17 victory and the league title. That thrilling contest—the first NFL championship game to be televised—helped make many new fans of pro football.

In 1959, the Colts again took on the Giants for the championship. The game was close until Unitas sparked the Colts to 24 fourth-quarter points, and Baltimore won in a 31–16 rout. This performance added to the already enormous legend of "Johnny U." "You can't intimidate him," said Los Angeles Rams defensive tackle Merlin Olsen. "He waits until the last possible second to release the ball, even if it means he's going to take a good lick. When he sees us coming, he knows it's going to hurt, and we know it's going to hurt. But he just stands there and takes it. No other quarterback has such class."

Quarterback Johnny Unitas was named the NFL's Most Valuable Player in 1959, 1964, and 1967.

IN THE FIRST few seasons of the 1960s, the Colts were a mediocre team. In 1963, Baltimore brought in Don Shula as its new head coach. Coach Shula's first step in boosting the Colts was to improve the defense. Although the team had several talented defenders, including linebacker Don Shinnick, it seemed to need a spark.

In 1965, Baltimore drafted hard-hitting linebacker Mike "Mad Dog" Curtis out of Duke University. Curtis made an immediate impact on the Colts—and on opposing players. "We were playing Green Bay," Baltimore linebacker Ted Hendricks later recalled. "[Packers running back] Jim Grabowski was coming through the line, and Mike Curtis gave him a good old-fashioned clothesline shot. Grabowski got up wobbly. One of our guys handed him his helmet. He started heading for our bench. I tapped him on the shoulder and turned him around and said, 'Yours is on the other side, Jim.'"

With Curtis heading the defense and Unitas guiding the offense, the Colts went 13–1 and won another NFL title in 1968 to advance to Super Bowl III. The Colts were heavily favored in the Super Bowl against the upstart New York Jets of the rival American Football League (AFL). But in one of the most famous upsets in sports history, the Jets and their star quarterback, Joe Namath, handed the Colts a 16–7 defeat.

The Colts returned to the Super Bowl two years later, this time to face the Dallas Cowboys. The Colts trailed 13–6 at halftime and found themselves without Unitas, who had been injured. But backup quarterback Earl Morrall led the offense down the field for a tying touchdown late in the fourth quarter, and Curtis then intercepted a Dallas pass. Three plays later, kicker Jim O'Brien booted a field goal to give the Colts a 16–13 win and their fourth NFL championship.

An aggressive tackler, linebacker Don Shinnick helped anchor Baltimore's defense for 12 seasons^

THE COLTS MADE the playoffs in 1971 but were beaten by the Miami Dolphins. That was the last hurrah for many of the great Colts players of the '60s. When the Colts finished the 1972 season 5–9, it was clear that the team needed some new talent. After the season, new team owner Robert Irsay decided to trade Unitas to the San Diego Chargers. Unitas left Baltimore as the NFL's all-time leader in pass completions (2,796), passing yards (39,768), and touchdown passes (287).

In 1973, the Colts found their new quarterback in the NFL Draft, selecting Louisiana State University star Bert Jones. The young quarterback spent his first two seasons on the bench, but by 1975, he was ready to step into the starting role. Jones proved to be a worthy replacement for Unitas by leading the Colts to a 10–4 record and their first American Football Conference (AFC) Eastern Division title.

Jones quickly earned the respect of his teammates with his leadership and toughness. In one
1976 game, he led the Colts to a victory over the
Houston Oilers despite having a terrible case of the
flu. "He was so sick yesterday that I thought he'd
fall down if an Oiler so much as breathed on him,"
said Baltimore offensive lineman George Kuntz after
the game. "But he played another great game. He's
tough…. It kind of rubs off on the rest of us."

With the help of speedy running back Lydell
Mitchell, Jones led the Colts to division titles
again in 1976 and 1977. Even though the Colts
lost in the first round of the playoffs both years,
Baltimore fans hoped that even better things were
just around the corner.

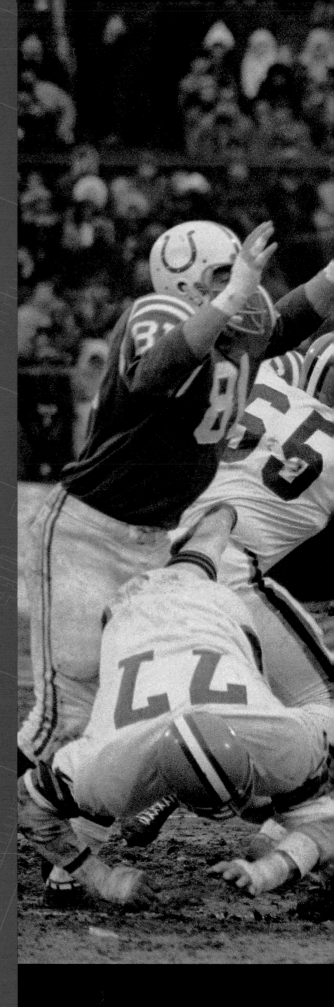

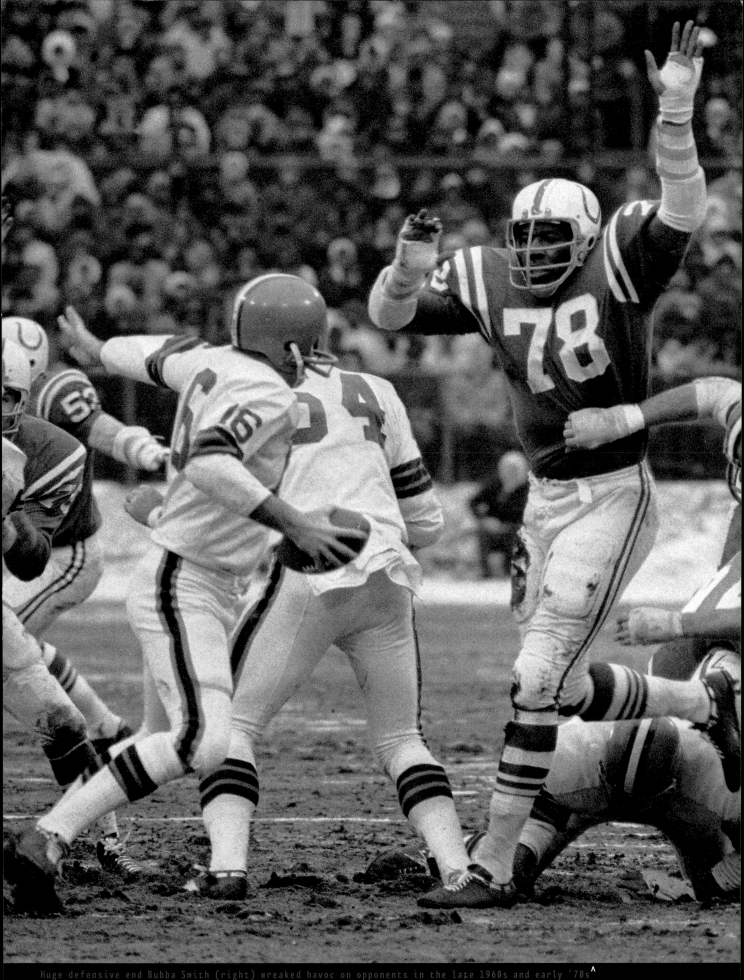

Huge defensive end Bubba Smith (right) wreaked havoc on opponents in the late 1960s and early '70s ^

FROM 1978 TO 1983, the Colts struggled, posting a losing record every year despite the best efforts of Pro Bowl running back Joe Washington. After the 1983 season, investors from Indianapolis approached Irsay about moving his team to their city. Irsay looked at Indianapolis's Hoosier Dome, a brand-new, 60,000-seat domed stadium, and decided to make the move. One night, moving vans showed up at the team's Baltimore headquarters, and the Colts bolted for Indiana.

The move broke the hearts of many faithful Baltimore fans, but sports fans in Indiana enthusiastically welcomed the team, even as it continued to struggle in the mid-1980s. Then, in 1987, the Colts traded for star running back Eric Dickerson. Known for his graceful yet hard-nosed running style, Dickerson had established himself as one of the league's top rushers with the Los Angeles Rams.

Known for his smooth

Dickerson joined a Colts offense that already featured deep-threat wide receiver Bill Brooks and outstanding linemen Ray Donaldson and Chris Hinton. This collection of players helped carry the 1987 Colts to a 9–6 record, an AFC East title, and their first playoff appearance in 10 years. "This year, it all came true," said Donaldson. "All the dreams we had before."

In 1988, Dickerson charged for a franchise-record 1,659 yards as the Colts went 9–7 and just missed the playoffs. But after that, Indianapolis began to stumble. Over the next two seasons, the Colts went 8–8 and 7–9. In 1991, the team collapsed completely with an embarrassing 1–15 record.

Fearless receiver Bill Brooks led the club in receptions for four seasons in the late 1980s and early '90s ^

IN 1992, TED MARCHIBRODA, who had coached the Colts in Baltimore in the 1970s, was hired to rebuild the franchise again. Marchibroda believed that coaching was "a 24-hour-a-day job. No motivating speech is going to make a difference. You have to work with your football team every minute to get it ready to play on Sunday."

Marchibroda's commitment paid off as the team jumped to 9–7 in 1992. The team slumped to 4–12 a year later, but Coach Marchibroda then made two key off-season moves that would give the team a major boost. First, he signed veteran quarterback Jim Harbaugh. Then, he drafted Marshall Faulk—an all-purpose running back known for his quick acceleration and shifty moves—in the first round of the 1994 NFL Draft.

In 1995, these players propelled the Colts back to the playoffs for a magical run. First, they upset the defending AFC champion San Diego Chargers 35–20. Then they beat the powerful Kansas City Chiefs 10–7. The excitement finally came to an end in the AFC championship game, when the Colts lost a 20–16 heartbreaker to the Pittsburgh Steelers. On the last play of the game, Harbaugh launched a "Hail Mary" pass that was nearly caught by Colts receiver Aaron Bailey for a touchdown.

The Colts again put together a 9–7 record and made the playoffs in 1996. A matchup against the Steelers in round one gave the Colts a chance to avenge the previous year's defeat, but the Steelers overwhelmed the Colts 42–14.

Jim Harbaugh threw a touchdown pass and nearly led the Colts to victory in the 1995 AFC title game.

WHEN THE COLTS slipped to 3–13 in 1997, the team was put in the hands of former New Orleans Saints head coach Jim Mora. With Mora at the helm, the Colts used the first overall pick in the 1998 NFL Draft to add a new quarterback: Peyton Manning, the son of former NFL quarterback Archie Manning.

In 1998, the Colts again went just 3–13. Manning, though, proved that he was something special by setting new NFL rookie records for passing yards (3,739) and pass completions (326). Many of those passes went to speedy wide receiver Marvin Harrison. "He's the kind of guy who wants to be coached," Coach Mora said of Manning. "You can't overwork him. He's like a sponge. He wants to do the best he can, and he wants you to give him all that you have to give him."

Quarterback Peyton Manning threw for more than 4,000 yards in five of his first six NFL seasons^

Known to fans and teammates as "Edge," Edgerrin James used a slashing, hard-nosed rushing style^

End Chad Bratzke made 12 quarterback sacks in 1999 ^

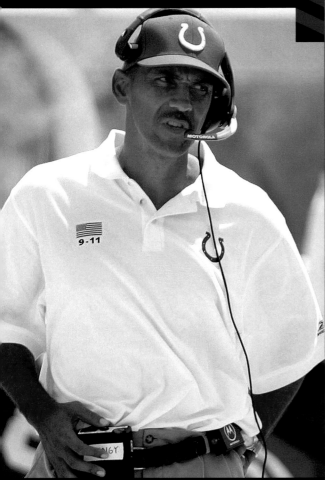

Tony Dungy was a soft-spoken but intense leader ^

With budding superstars at quarterback and wide receiver, the Colts continued to add talent. In 1999, they traded Marshall Faulk to the St. Louis Rams and then selected explosive University of Miami running back Edgerrin James in the NFL Draft. Indianapolis also built up its defense by signing veteran linebacker Cornelius Bennett and end Chad Bratzke.

The off-season moves paid off big-time as the Colts skyrocketed to a 13–3 record in 1999. Manning, Harrison, and James became perhaps the most feared offensive trio in the NFL: Manning threw for more than 4,000 yards, Harrison led all receivers with 1,663 yards, and James led the NFL in rushing with 1,553 yards. The season came to a disappointing end in the playoffs, though, as the Colts lost 19–16 to the Tennessee Titans.

When the Colts slumped to 6–10 in 2001, Coach Mora was replaced by Tony Dungy, a defense-minded coach who had previously built the Tampa Bay Buccaneers into a powerhouse. The Colts jumped to 10–6 in their first season under Dungy, thanks in part to rising star defensive end Dwight Freeney, receiver Reggie Wayne, and tight end Marcus Pollard. Harrison also made it a season to remember by catching an NFL-record 143 passes on the year.

The next year was even better, as Indianapolis surged to a 12–4 record and Manning was named the NFL's Most Valuable Player. The 2003 Colts charged all the way to the AFC championship game but came up just short of the Super Bowl, losing to the New England Patriots 24–14. Still, with Coach Dungy leading the "triplets" of Manning, Harrison, and James, the Colts were expected to remain an AFC heavyweight in 2004 and beyond.

The history of the Colts is a rich one that spans 50 years, includes two cities, and boasts four NFL championships. Over the years, fans in Baltimore have cheered on such legends as Raymond Berry and Johnny Unitas, and fans in Indianapolis have supported such stars as Eric Dickerson and Peyton Manning. Now, as they race into a new millennium, today's Colts plan to give Indiana's sports-crazy fans their first up-close look at a Super Bowl trophy.

INDEX>